SCIENCE
Magic
in the bedroom

SCIENCE Magic
in the bedroom

Richard Robinson

Illustrated by Alan Rowe

OXFORD

These books are dedicated to two households: firstly the one I grew up in,
where Dad, Mum, Anne, John and Philip were for ever dazzling their
gullible youngest with tricks like the ones here.
Secondly the household I got for myself later, with Morgan and Georgia
providing a new and demanding young audience for these same tricks.

OXFORD
UNIVERSITY PRESS

Great Clarendon Street, Oxford OX2 6DP

Oxford University Press is a department of the University of Oxford.
It furthers the University's objective of excellence in research, scholarship,
and education by publishing worldwide in

Oxford New York

Auckland Bangkok Buenos Aires Cape Town Chennai
Dar es Salaam Delhi Hong Kong Istanbul Karachi Kolkata
Kuala Lumpur Madrid Melbourne Mexico City Mumbai Nairobi
São Paulo Shanghai Taipei Tokyo Toronto

Oxford is a registered trade mark of Oxford University Press
in the UK and in certain other countries

British Library Cataloguing in Publication Data available

ISBN 0–19–911155-3

1 3 5 7 9 10 8 6 4 2

Printed in UK

CONTENTS

INTRODUCTION

All the tricks in this book are self-working – that means you don't have to be a great magician to do them. The 'magic' will be done by Nature.

Magic and science have a lot in common.

Both magic and science can produce wonderful effects that leave us gob-smacked. Audiences always want to work out how a magic illusion works. Scientists try equally hard to understand Nature's tricks,

Magicians use a lot of misdirection – getting the audience to look in one direction while the trick is being done in another; Nature often seems to be doing the same. For thousands of years we thought that the Sun travelled across the sky above us; now we know that the Sun stays put and we do the travelling, so the Sun only seems to move. That's Nature misdirecting us.

A magician's audiences will often say 'I know how that's done!', when in fact they've got it completely wrong. Scientists often make the same mistake. Two thousand years ago, the Greek philosopher Aristotle had some pretty wrong ideas. For instance, he thought that apples fell from trees because they wanted to. Aristotle's ideas seem crazy nowadays, but for 1500 years everyone thought he was the top banana!

Aristotle's mistakes have been corrected now, but some of the magic in these books still can't be explained even by the best of today's scientists; that makes it doubly magical.

As soon as a scientist finds that an experiment has gone wrong, he starts again, looking and testing and guessing until he gets it right. As you practice these tricks you'll find that they sometimes go wrong, but with a little practice you'll get them right. Soon your tricks will seem as magical to your audience as Nature seems to scientists.

Good luck.

Richard Robinson

CHAPTER ONE
TRICKS OF THE MIND

The first part of this book concerns the main thing in your bedroom – YOU! We'll see how easy it is for you to trick yourself, even when you know you're being tricked. You'll be seeing things that aren't there, and you'll be unable to see things that are right in front of your eyes.

Perhaps you think your bedroom is one place you can be completely alone. Think again. You are surrounded by strange creatures. The bugs that live in every corner of the room, the weird things that teem through your mind when you dream. Are there ghosts? What are those lights floating in front of your eyes? We will investigate.

Later on we're going to find hidden magic powers in the most unlikely places – a piece of paper, a lump of air, a plastic pen, a balloon . . .

All these things can give us ideas for magic illusions. But let's start with the impossible: doing amazing magic on yourself. That must seem as daft as trying to tickle yourself – it just can't work, can it? Well, as you will see, it can.

You're standing in your room. It's early evening. The light is beginning to fade outside. You turn on the light. Suddenly it's midnight! Outside, the sky has turned completely black. How did you get such power over nature? Whey aren't you famous? Why aren't you mobbed in the street?

Sorry, it's all rather boring, actually. Your eyes are playing tricks on you again.

They do this all the time, as we're going to see. In this particular case, the answer is neat, clear and visible. Find a mirror and watch your eyes in it while you turn the light on. The coloured bit of your eye, or **iris**, is actually a muscle. You can see it swell up and close off the hole into the eyeball (the **pupil**), to protect it from the light.

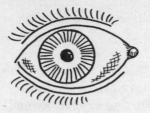

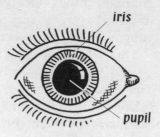

eye in bright light   *eye in dim light*

With less light going in, the bright things no longer dazzle, but the darker things, like the evening outside your window, are now even darker.

If too much light gets into the eye, the delicate light-sensitive cells (called the **retina**) get burned out. Take a quick glance at a bright light, then shut your eyes. That bright after-image that you see is the sign that some of the light-sensitive cells have been over-exposed. They get such a blast of light that they're still sending messages to the brain long after the light has gone. So, for a couple of minutes, you get great big bright blobs before your eyes.

One thing you must NOT EVER do is to stare directly at the Sun, because it is bright enough to do you lasting damage.

One thing you MUST do is use this after-image in a magic trick.

Oooh, it's soooo bright...

Put The Birdy In The Cage

THE EFFECT
The magician makes a ghostly bird appear in a cage.

YOU NEED
- Pen
- Paper

SECRET PREPARATION
Either use the bird and cage design here, or ask a print shop for a copy of it.

TO PERFORM

Ask someone to get the bird into the cage without touching it. It shouldn't take them more than a micro-second to realise this is impossible.

But for the magician, impossible it ain't!

Tell your assistant to cover one eye and stare at the bird's eye with the other. Let them keep staring for half a minute. Meanwhile give them a little patter along the lines of: *'Concentrate on the bird's eye. Stare into its eye. You are absorbing the bird's essence. Its very soul is now at your command . . . Now stare at the dot in the middle of the cage. There's the bird!'*

And there it is, for although you can't see it, your victim can clearly see the ghost of a black bird inside the cage.

WHAT HAPPENED

Scientists are still scratching their heads over these negative after-images. Your eye is constantly transmitting to the brain. Even when it's pitch black, there is still a background 'noise' of retina signals. It seems that when you stare so fixedly for so long at the white bird on the black square, some of your 'black and white' retina cells get exhausted, so that when you look away, they fail to send any signals at all, and you 'see' the opposite image floating in front of you – spooky! The eye is a complicated piece of work!

noise

THE OPTIC NERVE

For sure, the eye is a phenomenal mechanism, but it has one big problem, a problem which gives you the chance to play thousands of tricks on yourself and on an audience.

The problem is that although there are 180 million retina cells in the eye receiving light from outside, there is only a tiny optic nerve sending messages from there to your brain. As you can imagine, there's not enough cable space. So the information is coded and simplified, before being sent to the vision zone of the brain (the **visual cortex**). This then expands the message, filling in the gaps as best it can.

And that's why we can fox it.

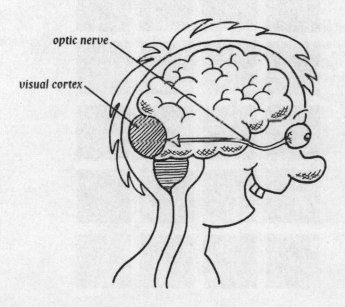

optic nerve

visual cortex

Eye Tweakers

All these illusions work because the brain receives confusing messages coming along the optic nerve from the eye, and tries to construct the most sensible picture it can, poor thing.

SPOTS BEFORE THE EYES

Who put the grey smudges between the black squares? You did! Look at any one of them closely and it will vanish.

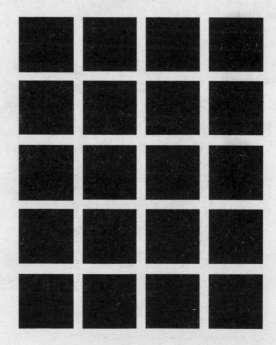

STRAIGHT AND WOBBLY

All the lines of the triangle are straight, even though your brain tells you they're curved.

SQUIFFY

All these lines are **parallel** (they all go straight up, at equal distances apart), but they actually seem to be leaning over every which way.

NOTION OF MOTION

Hold this picture up in front of your face and wobble it rapidly. The wheels appear to go round.

BEND AND STRETCH

Your brain can't help it; no matter how hard you tell yourself that these lines are straight and parallel, your mind sees them bending.

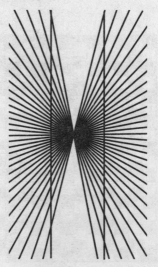

HOW FAR?

Which is the greater, the distance from A to B or from C to D? They're actually the same, although you can't believe it.

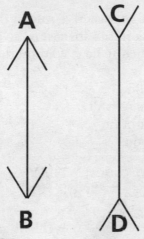

LITTLE AND LARGE

Which of the inner squares is larger? Again, they're the same, but you can't help thinking the white one is bigger.

BRAIN TWEAKERS

The brain takes a more active role in these mind-warping illusions, filling in the spaces in the pictures from the eye. You can practically hear your brain changing gear!

Can you see the triangles in this picture? There isn't even one, but your brain provides two for you.

Is this flight of stairs the right way up or upside down? Your mind can think one thing, then the other, but never both at the same time.

Are you looking at this table from above or from below? Once again, when the brain changes its opinion, the table changes position.

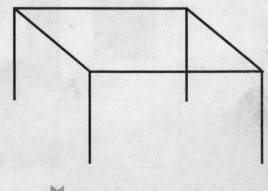

Why do you think this snail is breaking the speed limit?
Cartoonists use strange codes to indicate movements,
which your brain translates into the impression of speed.

How many cubes do you see here, six or seven? Both

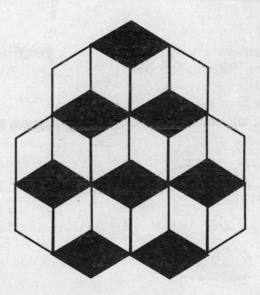

answers are correct, depending on how you look at it.
Here is a picture of two faces . . . or is it a candlestick?
Both are possible.

Some illusions are invisible to
people from different cultures.
Most Chinese people won't see
the letter E here, because they
never normally come across Es.

Where's the missing
slice of pie? Turn the book
upside down to see it.

What was solid now looks empty
and empty has become solid.

COLOURFUL LANGUAGE

The brain can seriously meddle with the eye's messages. Here a simple job for the eye becomes a nightmare for the mind.

THE EFFECT
A list of words becomes strangely difficult to say.

YOU NEED
- Two pieces of white paper
- Felt-tip pens – red, blue, yellow, green, purple, orange and brown

SECRET PREPARATION
Use the felt-tip pens to make two lists of words, as below. Use a different colour to write each word. In particular, in the list of colours, use the 'wrong' colour pens (for instance, don't use a red pen to write the word RED, use perhaps green the first time and blue the second)

TREE	BROWN
HORSE	RED
BUSH	BLUE
CAR	ORANGE
DOG	PURPLE
TABLE	BLUE
CARPET	YELLOW
PLANE	BROWN
BALL	GREEN
KING	RED

TO PERFORM

Pick on a grown-up. Tell them this is a very simple colour spotting test. You have a list of ten words written in different colours, and you want them to tell you the colour of each word, at the rate of one a second.

As an example, produce the first list and recite the colour of each word at about the right speed.

When they're good and ready, give them the second list to read out and watch them flounder. They'll stumble and stutter, and often get the colour wrong altogether.

WHAT HAPPENED

The visual cortex has got a simple enough task to identify the colour, but another message keeps interrupting. From other parts of the brain come these nagging calls:

Confusion is unavoidable.

EYE DON'T BELIEVE IT!

Scientists are trying to understand why we are so easily confused by optical illusions. Here are a couple of their explanations. Do you think they're right?

NEAR AND FAR

In this drawing, the two figures are the same size. Why does one look bigger than the other?

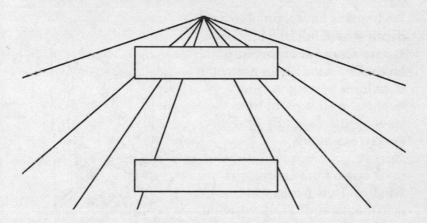

Your brain sees the radiating lines and decides that you are looking along a road disappearing into the distance. As you know, objects look smaller when they're farther away. Since these two oblongs appear the same size, that must mean that the farther one is bigger. The brain 'sees' it accordingly.

SCARED OF DEPTH

Which line is longer, the flat one or the upright one? They're both the same length, yet your mind won't let you believe it.

We humans have a problem with depth – we don't like it. We are always scared of falling into holes. Our minds help protect us from birth by exaggerating depths. So all upright lines that we look at are slightly exaggerated in our minds.

Look down from an upstairs window. How far do you think it is to the ground? Find out with a piece of string. Now measure out the same distance along the street. Does it seem the same?

STRETCHING THE POINT

Here's a trick based on another optical illusion. This one foxes the audience again and again, and scientists can't explain why.

THE EFFECT
The magician just can't get two pieces of cardboard to stay the same size.

YOU NEED
- Two pieces of cardboard
- Scissors
- Paper

SECRET PREPARATION
Trace the design below on to paper.

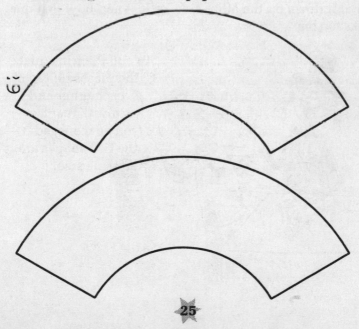

With the paper on top of the two pieces of card, cut round the shape, so that you end up with two identical curved pieces of card. Decorate them.

TO PERFORM
Place the two pieces side by side, and ask the audience which is smaller.

When they show you, tell them that you will make this smaller piece of card the same size as its partner by magically stretching it. Pick it up, pretend to stretch it, then put it down on the other side of its partner. Oh no! You've stretched it too far – it's now too big. Pick up the new 'smaller' one and stretch it. Put it down on the other side again – and now that one looks too big.

To end the trick, place the pieces on top of each other and show that at last you've managed it – the two shapes are the same size!

POT LUCK DUCK

THE EFFECT
The magician makes a rabbit turn into a duck.

YOU NEED
• Large envelope
• Picture like the one below.
  (Trace it with the help of some tracing paper.)

TO PERFORM
Here's the patter and the
actions to perform.

*'Rebecca goes into a pet shop
and says, "I would like to buy
a rabbit, please." Roger, the pet
shop man, says, "Certainly!
Here's a robust rabbit, called
Robert."*

Show the rabbit picture.

*"Shall I wrap Robert
rabbit, Rebecca? says
Roger." "I have a
reliable rabbit
wrapping robot."*

"Yes please," says Rebecca.

'So Roger makes the robot rabbit wrapper wrap Robert the robust rabbit for Rebecca.'

Put the picture in the envelope.

'Rebecca takes it home, but imagine her shock when she unwraps the robot rabbit wrapper's wrappings. She's been diddled – it's a duck!'

Take the picture out again – this time on its side, to look like a duck.

WHAT HAPPENED

All sorts of memories and calculations went into concluding that the first drawing was a rabbit. . . long things on top of head = rabbit. When the picture was rotated, the same mental mechanisms judged, 'long things on front of head = duck.'

DOTS INCREDIBLE!

*O*nce again, the brain over-reaches itself.

THE EFFECT
The magician has one card with four faces.

YOU NEED
- Postcard-sized piece of card or paper, blank on both sides
- Pen

SECRET PREPARATION
Draw dots on the card as in the pictures below.

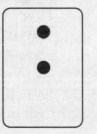 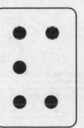

TO PERFORM
To begin with, keep the card out of view.

Say, '*I have here a four-faced card. It's got four dots on the first face . . .*'
Hold the card up in your left hand, with your fingers covering one of the five dots.

Now hold it up with your fingers covering one of the two dots and say, '*It's got one dot on the second face...*'

Now show the five dot face, with your fingers covering the space, and say, '*... six dots on the third face ...*'

Do the same with the two dot face and say, '*and three dots on the fourth face!*'

WHAT HAPPENED

So long as you do it pretty quickly, the audience has no time to think about things too hard; their brain makes up what their eye can't see.

In the first case, they see four dots – nothing wrong with that. In the second case, one dot – OK so far.

In the third case, things get more interesting. They expect to see a symmetrical drawing, so they guess that a sixth dot lies under your fingers. The same with the last face; they can't believe that two dots would sit like that unless there was another under your fingers.

THE DOT THAT'S NOT

Did you know that part of your eye is making it all up? There's a patch which can't see anything, and you never ever notice. Here's a trick that shows it up.

THE EFFECT
The magician makes a dot disappear before your very eyes.

YOU NEED
• This page, or a copy of the picture shown below on a piece of paper.

X   ●

TO PERFORM
Tell your victim that the sign of a true magician is the ability to make things disappear. Luckily you have this skill, and here's proof.

Hold the diagram up about 30 cm in front of their face. Tell them to cover their left eye and stare at the cross. They will see the dot out of the corner of their eye. Slowly move the picture towards their right eye, saying, '*Tell me when the dot has gone. Dot, you are not . . . Dot, you are not . . .* 'At about 20 cm your victim will report the disappearance of the dot.

WHAT HAPPENED

Where the optic nerve leaves the eye for the brain, there is a **blind spot** with no light-sensitive retina cells.

optic nerve

blind spot

So the brain constantly guesses what's going on, using the information from surrounding cells. When the dot's image is exactly over the blind spot, the surrounding cells have nothing to say, so the brain guesses there's nothing there. Out of sight, out of mind!

There are many other things the brain takes liberties with. For instance, you can't see the nose in front of your face! The brain plain ignores it. Put a blob of white paint on it and suddenly your brain will start recording it continuously – 'What's that thing in the corner of my vision? . . . It's still there . . . It's following me around . . . ' and so on, joined, no doubt, by a chorus of 'Wipe your nose!' from parents and teachers.

The biggest, brashest thing your brain does is to turn the entire picture on its head. The easiest way to show why, is to build a **camera obscura**.

CAMERA OBSCURA

The name comes from Latin: 'obscura' means dark, and 'camera' means a small room. The original camera was just that – a small, dark room.

Hundreds of years ago (when all educated people spoke Latin), some poor misbehaving monk was flung into this room as a punishment. When his eyes had adjusted to the gloom (see page 9) he noticed it was not all dark; there was a tiny hole in the window shutter. He couldn't see much when he pressed his eye to it. But a little while later he noticed, on the wall opposite, a dim picture of the scene outside. He could watch the world pass by just by gazing at the wall – mediaeval television! There was only one small problem; the image was upside down.

You can make your own camera obscura without the hassle of learning Latin or getting flung into prison. Just cut the back off a shoe box, stick a screen of tissue paper or cooking parchment across the gap, pierce the opposite side with a thick pin or skewer, cover yourself over with a coat to cut out all light (so that your eyes can adjust to the dark) and point the hole towards the window. There will be a perfect upside down picture of the window projected on the screen.

It's even easier if you have a magnifying glass; take it to the darkest part of the room and hold it up facing the window, with a piece of paper behind it. With the right distance between the two, the window will be faithfully projected on to the paper.

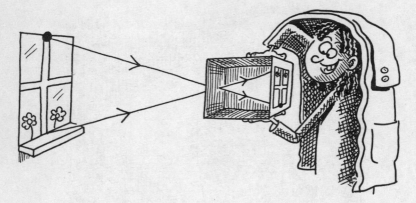

All these pictures are upside down, and the same is true of the picture in your own eye. Clearly the brain does a massive recalculation to arrive at the image we see of the world, the right way up.

A century ago a scientist built himself a pair of goggles that turned the image on his retina round the 'proper' way. He spent the next month coping with a world which seemed completely topsy-turvy. Flights of stairs seemed to plummet downwards below him when they were actually going up. Plates of food hovered over his head, but he still had to grope downwards to touch them.

After about four weeks, though, his brain adjusted, and he was able to get about as well as before. Then he took the goggles off, and the trouble started all over again, in reverse!

CHAPTER TWO

How Touching

It isn't just your eyes that can be tricked. Here are four ways to fox your own touch senses.

FINGER FOXING

Cross your arms over in front of you, turn your hands inwards, clasp fingers and bend the hands back and up in front of your chest, as in the drawings. Now ask someone to point (without touching) to one of your fingers. Can you move it? Your brain mixes up its messages and loses its way around your own body.

WRITING BACKWARDS

Do this quickly or you won't fool your body for long enough. Put a piece of paper on your forehead and write FORWARDS on it. When you look, you'll find that you've written FORWARDS backwards.

IT'S OUT OF YOUR HANDS

To do this next trick, follow the drawings as if they were a mirror.

Hold out your hand, palm up.

Raise the hand straight up to your shoulder.

Pass it down across your chest.

Swing it back out in front.

Raise it up to your shoulder, as before.

And pass it down across your chest, as before.

And swing it out in front as before . . . only different! Your hand is now palm down.

WHAT NERVE!

You need two pencils for this – sharp, but not too sharp.

Ask someone to close their eyes. Now touch the skin on their hands with both pencil points at the same time, about 1 cm apart. Ask them how many points they feel. Do it again with the points a little closer, and continue until they can feel only one point.

Try it at different places: upper arm, fingertip, and then – the big one – try it on their back. You'll find that there you can have the pencil points up to 2 cm apart and still they feel only one point.

You have fewer touch nerves on your back, spread out quite thinly. It is much more important to know what's happening at your fingertips so you have millions of nerves there.

PURE LUCK

You use your extra-sensitive fingers in this trick.

THE EFFECT
When tossing a coin, the magician is able to predict heads or tails every time.

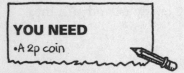

YOU NEED
•A 2p coin

TO PERFORM
The audience needs a little softening up for this trick. Talk to them about coin tossing; how impossible it is to tell whether it's heads or tails on every go. In fact, you expect to guess correctly about half the time.

Now start tossing and guessing.

Always catch the coin with one hand, then slap it down on the back of the other one, as in the drawing.

The trick happens just after you catch it. Your thumb strokes the back of the coin. Heads are smoother than tails. Your thumb's millions of nerves can tell the tiny difference.

You guess correctly every time.

CATCH AS CATCH CAN

This is a trick which shows how slowly the brain works.

THE EFFECT
People are unable to grab a book even when it is dangled between their fingers.

YOU NEED
•This book

TO PERFORM
Perform this over the bed, to protect the book from being damaged. All that anyone has to do is catch the book.

Hold the book between their thumb and fingers, the bottom of the book level with their thumb. As soon as you let go of the book, they can grab for it.

It seems easy enough, but they can't do it. The book always drops though their hand before they can touch it.

WHAT HAPPENED

This trick shows you a little about how the brain works. This is what happens:

1 eye sees the hand letting go of the book
2 eye sends message to visual cortex of brain – ' Book released.'
3 visual cortex sends message to muscle control centre – 'Go for it!'
4 muscle control centre sends message to hand – 'Go for it!'
5 hand muscles make a grab
6 eye sends message to visual cortex – 'Missed!'
7 visual cortex informs speech centre
8 speech centre sends message to mouth and breathing muscles
9 mouth says, 'Hang on, I wasn't ready! Give me one more go.'

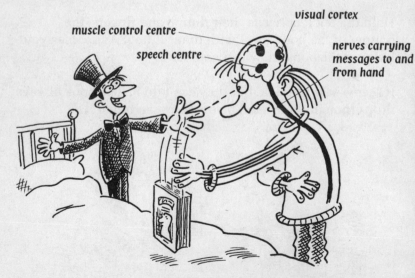

To get from 1 to 5 takes ⅓ of a second, longer than the book takes to drop through their fingers.

CHAPTER THREE

HEARING THINGS

The ear's ability to get it wrong has a whole branch of show biz dedicated to it. Puppets only get away with their simple mouth flappings because the audience enters into a sort of plot with the puppeteer to believe that the dolls are really talking.

HOW TO DEE A ZENTRILOQUIST

Say that title without moving your lips. It isn't too hard, if you can avoid saying the few sounds that force your lips to move.

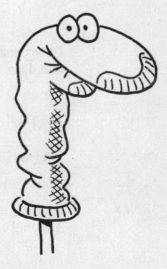

Instead of B use a soft D sound.

Instead of F use a Th sound.

Instead of M use a N sound.

Instead of P use a soft T sound.

Instead of V use a soft Th sound.

Instead of W use a soft R sound.

Make a simple puppet out of a sock. As long as your lips aren't moving, the audience will watch the puppet. To help the illusion out, look at the puppet too when it talks to you. So now you're ready to perform.

YOU	*Ladies and gentlemen,* *may I present Stinky the Sock.*
	(Produce Stinky.)
STINKY	*Don't call ne 'Stinky!'*
YOU	*Why not? You are stinky. Pooooo!*
	(Push Stinky away.)
STINKY	*Well, it's your theet that nake ne stink.* *Anyway, I know what to do.*
YOU	Go on.
STINKY	*Ith you don't like the snell, don't stick ne on* *your theet!*

YOU	*Good idea, Stinky!*
STINKY	*Can I go on a holiday then?*
YOU	*No, if I'm not going to wear you, I don't need you anymore. You can go in the dustbin.*
STINKY	*Oh no! Don't throw ne aray. How sad I an! Ooooh!*
	(Stinky leaves, sobbing sadly.)
YOU	*Oh dear, I've upset him . . . OK, Stinky, you can stay if you like.*
	(Stinky rushes back, happy again.)
STINKY	*Oh thank you! Thank you! Thank you!*
	(Stinky jumps up and licks you all over.)
YOU	*Ugh! No! Pooagh! Yuk!*

MAGIC MATCHBOX

A virtual ventriloquist trick.

THE EFFECT
The magician can make a full matchbox empty, and an empty one full!

> **YOU NEED**
> • Three matchboxes
> – one full, two empty
> • Elastic band
> • Long sleeves

SECRET PREPARATION
Use the elastic band to fix the full matchbox under your left wrist. Cover it with your sleeve.

Now when you shake an empty matchbox with your left hand it seems full, and with your right hand it seems empty.

hidden matchbox

rattle

TO PERFORM

Show the two empty matchboxes to your audience and say, *'Here, ladies and gentlemen, I have two matchboxes. The one on my left is full . . . '* (pick up the left matchbox in your left hand and shake it) *' . . . but the one on the right is empty'* (shake the right box with the right hand).

'The problem is how to get the matches from the left-hand matchbox . . .' (rattle the left-hand box again with the left hand) *' . . . into the right-hand matchbox'* (shake the right-hand box again with the right hand).

'I could do it by moving the right-hand box to the left and the left-hand box to the right . . . ' (do this) *' . . . and then this box becomes empty . . .'* (shake the right-hand box with the right hand) *' . . . but so does this one'* (shake the left-hand box with the RIGHT hand).

'Or I could move the left-hand box which was the right-hand box, just to the right of the right-hand box which was the left-hand box, so the left becomes right and the right becomes left, right? Or have I left you right behind?' (Move the boxes back, then swap them again, and add in a couple of confusing moves.)

'*Now, which one is full? Is it this one? . . .*' (rattle the left-hand box with the left hand). '*Or this one? . . .*' (shake the right-hand box with the right hand).

Let the audience tell you it's the left-hand box, then say, '*Well, it can't be this one . . .*' (shake the left-hand box with the RIGHT hand) '*. . . so it must be this one!*' (Rattle the right-hand box with the LEFT hand.)

Finally, say, '*Actually, I cheated. They're both full!*' (Rattle both with the left hand, then throw them to the audience.) '*So you can have one box, and you can have the other!*'

When they check, of course, both boxes are empty.

WHAT HAPPENED
There is only one explanation the audience can believe: obviously, you really are magic!

CHAPTER FOUR

GHOST HUNT

Are you, or were you ever, scared of the dark? After the lights go out, do mysterious shapes move in the corner and give you the heeby-jeebies? After the last few chapters you probably have an idea where they come from. Shadows in your bedroom can play tricks with your imagination. But what about things that go BONK in the night?

Late at night and early in the morning, most houses are haunted by clunking sounds. The cause might indeed be the steady tramp of the murderous pirate with a wooden leg who, 200 years ago, throttled an entire family in the very bed you're sleeping in. But it's more likely to be the central heating. When the pipes warm up, they expand slightly and rub against the floor-boards.

So now you can sleep at ease, reassured that the sounds that you can hear have a simple scientific explanation.

The 20,000 creatures who creep around your room at night are mostly silent.

TWENTY THOUSAND?!

CREEPY CRAWLIES

Actually, 20,000 is a little out – it's more like 20 million creatures. And it's hardly surprising. Your bedroom is a very desirable residence indeed. Nicely snug and warm all year round, with a constant rain of food from the heavens for the herds of animals which roam around the carpet all day and share your bed all night. There are around 2 million in your bed with you, and 4 or 5 million in the carpet and furnishings.

They are, of course, **dust mites**: microscopic creatures so small that their existence was only discovered in 1965. They are related to spiders and have the same features: eight legs, claws, a mouth and an appetite. Dust mites eat human flesh – but don't worry, they aren't out to get you. There's no need. A continuous avalanche of human flesh falls from the sky as household dust, half of which is flakes of skin which are constantly being rubbed off you as you move about. All a dust mite has to do is just wait in the carpet for a gigantic pizza of skin to plop in front of it. That will be breakfast, lunch and supper for the next few days.

Apart from the dust mites, you shouldn't forget these . . .
You'll never feel lonely again!

FLOATERS

Sometimes you see transparent
worms floating past your eyes.
These are not creatures,
though they often look
like them. They're called
floaters, and are minute
bits of waste from
inside your eye, drifting
about in the liquid
between your lens and
retina. Because they are
very close to the retina,
they seem enormous, but
they're actually microscopic.

REAL NIGHTMARES

Apart from the real creatures in your room, there are the
imaginary ones – the ones that parade through your mind
when you sleep.

Everybody dreams for at least a ¼ of every night. Not
everyone remembers them, and nobody knows why we do
it, but we do know that you can't do without them. People
who are stopped from having dream-sleep suffer terrible
mental torment.

But why is dreaming so vital? Perhaps it is part of a
process of sorting out today's thoughts and events ready
for the next period of wakefulness tomorrow.

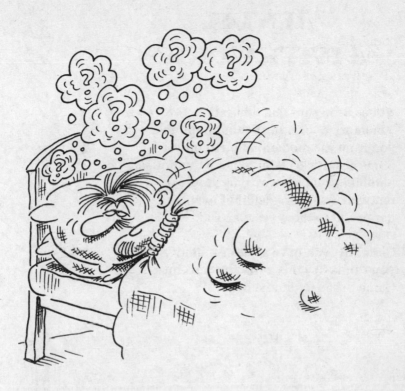

Dreams show you the enormous complexity of the human brain, and how difficult it is to, as it were, get your mind around it. One researcher has explained that if the human brain were simple enough for us to understand it, we'd be so simple that we couldn't!

The brain never stops. It is constantly monitoring you and the world around you; planning, judging, storing or calculating. It uses about a ⅕ of all the energy you use, and it's got a terrific memory.

CHAPTER FIVE

MENTAL MASTERWORKS

It has been said that you retain a memory of everything that happens to you from the moment of birth onwards. Some scientists claim to have hypnotised patients in such a way that they remembered every detail of events that happened to them years ago.

Certainly, you have a better memory than you think. Try this variation on Kim's Game to see for yourself.

✳ **Magic** ✳

KIM'S GAME

Here are 30 objects. Run your eye along the rows and try to memorise all of them, but only allow yourself one second for each picture. (Don't worry if you don't think they're going in.)

When you've done this, turn the page. You don't think you can remember them all, do you?

Have a look at the pictures below. One of them was not among the collection on the last page. Can you spot which one?

If you can, you were tapping into your **recognition memory**, a special department of your memory store. Normally you have to use **recall memory**, which is not usually so clever.

Nobody enjoys trying to remember lists of things, but there are memory tricks that can be used, called **mnemonics** (see the next page).

MIGHTY MEMORY MNEMONICS

Your memory powers will amaze even you!

THE EFFECT
The magician can remember a list of ten words and recall them at will.

YOU NEED
A mnemonic, or trick to help your memory. For this bit of magic, use a list of words that rhyme with the numbers 1 to 10, such as:

one	bun
two	shoe
three	tree
four	door
five	dive
six	sticks
seven	heaven
eight	plate
nine	mine
ten	hen

TO PERFORM
Ask someone in the audience to write out a list of ten objects, then recite them to you quite slowly. Mentally, attach each object to your mnemonic list in an interesting way. For instance, if the list were: coat, ship, spaghetti, bottle, flower, dog, scissors, hair, toffee, bed; your mental pictures might look like this . . .

Now, when your volunteer asks you any question about their list, you have the answer. If they ask you what number three is, you remember 'tree' and the picture comes straight out. This mnemonic will be useful for the rest of your life.

CHAPTER SIX

Mathemagical Miracles

Now that the world has discovered your extraordinary mental powers, it's time to impress them with your phenomenal ability to know each and every card in a pack.

Actually, these card tricks are all self-working. They make use of simple mathematical skulduggery to fool the audience.

THE NUMBER NINE FORCE

In card tricks, a 'force' is what magicians use to make you 'freely' pick a card of their choice.

Position the card you want your victim to choose at number nine. Hand the cards to the volunteer, ask them to think of a number between (but not including) 10 and 20, and count off that many cards from the top, one at a time.

Ask your victim to add together the two digits of the number. So if they chose 13, they add 1 and 3 to get 4. They then take the small packet they just dealt and count that many cards off the top. Tell them to memorise the next card. This one is your card!

The maths is very simple, though they don't know it. If you add the digits together and subtract form the original number, the answer is always nine.

$$11 - 2 = 9$$
$$12 - 3 = 9$$
$$13 - 4 = 9$$
$$14 - 5 = 9$$
$$15 - 6 = 9$$
$$16 - 7 = 9$$
$$17 - 8 = 9$$
$$18 - 9 = 9$$
$$19 - 10 = 9$$

CARTESIAN CARDS

This is as easy as reading a map . . . oh all right then, it's as difficult as reading a map!

Lay 25 cards out, face-up, in five columns of five.

Now, I don't want to get picky about style, but the way you handle these cards out is important. You must deal them *across* the array, but pick them up column by column, i.e., *up* the array.

Ask someone secretly to select a card, then tell you only which column it's in.

Collect the cards up (column by column, remember),

making sure the selected column is the middle one.
Lay the cards down again (row by row, remember) – the columns have now become rows and their column is the third row.
Ask which column the chosen card is in now.
Collect the cards again, with the chosen column in the middle again. Your volunteer's card is now in the middle of the pack – card number 13.

Now for the climax. Hold the cards face down and deal each one out in turn, feeling the 'aura' of each one in your search. When you get to card number 13, say, *'I sense that this is it. What was the name of your card?'*

When they tell you, turn over their card. Amazing!

NICE DICE

Here's a trick which relies on a little-known fact about dice – the opposite faces on a die add up to seven. In this one, the magician shows he has X-ray vision! He can see right through a pile of dice.

All you need is three dice. Turn your back. Ask someone to throw the dice, then pile them into a column.

Tell them that understanding the human mind is hard enough, but understanding dice is even harder – they're completely dotty. None-the-less, you will try to read these dice's thoughts, and tell everyone how many dots there are in the middle of the column, hidden from view.

Ask your volunteer to add up the dots on the top and bottom and tell you the total. Without turning round, you can tell them the sum of the dots in the middle!

It's easy. The top and bottom of each die adds up to seven. Three times that is 21, which is the total for all the middle dots. Subtracting your volunteer's total from 21 gives you the sum of the hidden dots.

CHAPTER SEVEN

Static, But Not Still

If you take your clothes off in the dark when you're getting ready for bed, you can sometimes see tiny sparks of light in the middle of your shirt or pullover. The cause of these mini-lightning flashes are going to be your assistants in the next few tricks. They are **electrons**, tiny weeny, minute, minuscule, unbelievably titchy particles which hum around in the universe. Small – yes, but useless – no. When vast masses of them go streaming down a wire, we call it electricity. When they are shot from a special gun at a special kind of glass screen, we call it TV.

Some substances, such as plastic or nylon, seem to act as electron hoovers. They suck electrons off surrounding objects. The extra electrons attract or push away (repel) nearby objects. This force is called static electricity.

Sometimes the electrons jump across gaps with a spark and a click. You can occasionally feel this as a tiny electric shock on cars or in some buildings.

Sometimes the electric shock is not so tiny . . .

LORD OF THE SKIES

Lightning flashes are the result of electrons jumping in a mass across the gaps between clouds and the Earth. Thunder is the sound made by the flashes. Here's how to create your own thunder storm!

YOU NEED
- Any clothing (such as pullovers, sheets, dresses) with a lot of acrylic (plastic) in them. These are your clouds.

TO PERFORM
On a dry night, shut your bedroom door and pull the curtains, so your room is completely dark. When your eyes have fully adjusted to the dark (it takes at least five minutes), begin shuffling the clothes around, rubbing them against your hair and against each other. You will probably see some flashes of lightning and hear some tiny crackles (thunder!).

WHAT HAPPENED
As you rub the clothing, electrons are being scraped off one part and then being recaptured from another part. Mostly this happens very easily, but sometimes the electrons have to leap through the air to get from one place to another. The flashes and crackles are made as they jump.

Lord Of The Lightning

If you want to be more in control of the lightning, this is the right trick for you.

THE EFFECT
The magician can make lightning flashes at will.

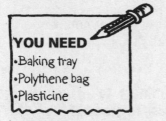

YOU NEED
• Baking tray
• Polythene bag
• Plasticine

SECRET PREPARATION
To give this the best performance, grown a long beard, put on flowing robes and descend from the clouds in a chariot drawn by six magic horses.

TO PERFORM
You are the new god of thunder! You will create a bolt of lightning and fling it at anyone you choose! Pick your victim.

Reassure them that it won't hurt too much. In fact, you'd do this yourself, only you're feeling a little Thor today.

Push the plasticine into the baking tray so that you can pick it up without touching the metal. (This will retain the electric charge.)

Spread the polythene bag out and rub the tray up and down it a few times, then bring it close to the victim's fingertip. A spark will jump across the gap, accompanied by a small click. (Well, you're not in the big time yet, but remind them this lightning comes almost completely free of 'charge'.)

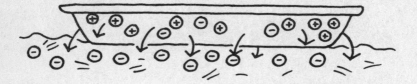

WHAT HAPPENED
The plastic rubbed electrons off the tray, which then attracted replacement electrons from the victim's finger. When the electrons jumped across the gap, the victim felt a small shock.

PAPER BALLET

Tear up some toilet paper into tiny pieces – the smaller, the better. Place a few inside an empty cassette case and rub the outside with your sleeve. The paper pieces will perform a ballet inside the case.

As you rub, the plastic picks up electrons from your sleeve. This creates an electro–static charge on the top, and the paper is attracted towards it.

WATER MAGNET

Your power need not be confined to paper . . .

THE EFFECT
The magician can make water bend to his will.

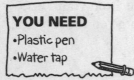

YOU NEED
• Plastic pen
• Water tap

TO PERFORM
Tell the audience that you can bend water by sheer willpower.

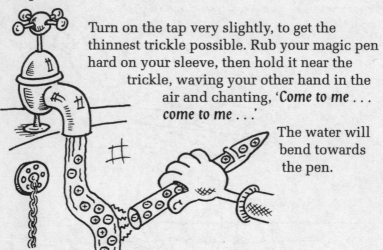

Turn on the tap very slightly, to get the thinnest trickle possible. Rub your magic pen hard on your sleeve, then hold it near the trickle, waving your other hand in the air and chanting, '*Come to me . . . come to me . . .*'

The water will bend towards the pen.

WHAT HAPPENED
The penful of electrons attracted the water in the same way as the paper was attracted in the last trick.

MAGICAL MIND MAKER-UPPER

This is an excellent trick using static electricity.

THE EFFECT
The magician demonstrates a new gizmo – a magical mind maker-upper.

YOU NEED
- £1 coin
- Small piece of paper, about 1 cm x 2 cm
- Two felt-tip pens

PREPARATION
Draw an arrow on the paper and balance it on the edge of the coin, as in the picture.

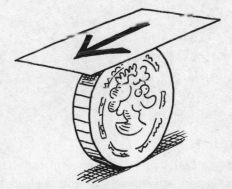

TO PERFORM

Set up the paper and coin, hold one pen in each hand, then say, *'Sometimes you need to make your mind up – shall I do it . . . shall I not do it? You could toss a coin to make up your mind. But why be old fashioned? Tossing coins is yesterday's technology. With the all new, patented, mystical, magical mind maker-upper you need never again face a problem unprotected.*

'The arrow will tell you what to do. If it points left, it means "no". If it points right it means "yes".

'Simply rub the magic plastic pens of the oracle on your clothes, like so . . .' (do it) *' . . . bring them towards the arrow from either side . . . '* (bring the pens towards the front edges of the arrow as you speak) *' . . . and whatever the arrow guides you to do, do it!'*

The arrow will swing to the left or right. Your mind has been made up.

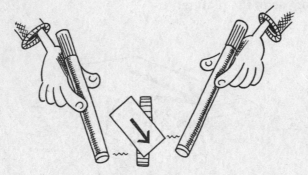

WHAT HAPPENED

As the electro-statically charged pens approach the paper, both are attracting it, but the one which is slightly closer will attract it just that little bit more. The paper will swing that way.

SHOCKER

THE EFFECT
The magician has something in a magic bag which will make the audience's hair stand on end.

YOU NEED
- Pullover with sleeves drawn in so that it looks like a bag.
- A blown-up balloon inside the 'bag'.

TO PERFORM
Practise looking dangerous and menacing to give this trick the best effect.

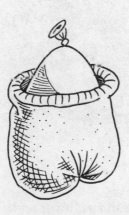

Prowl about the audience, choosing your victim. Pick on someone with long straight hair. Tell them, *'I have something in my magic bag which will make your hair stand on end. Would you like to see it?'*

Before they have time to answer, pull the balloon quickly out of the bag and hold it above their head. Their hair will stand on end!

WHAT HAPPENED

The balloon rubbed some electrons off the pullover and became charged. The hair was attracted towards it.

BALLOON TRAINER

THE EFFECT
When the magician tells a balloon to stop dropping, it stops dropping.

YOU NEED
- Balloon
- Wastebasket

TO PERFORM
Arrange the basket against a blank piece of wall. Hold the balloon about 1 m above it and ask the audience if it will drop into the basket when you let it go. They may think there's a catch (puh-leeze!) and say it won't drop in.

Hold it 50 cm above the basket and ask the same. Hold it 20 cm above and ask the same. Hold it 5 cm above the basket. Surely no one's in any doubt by now. When you let go of the balloon, it'll drop straight in.

Rub the balloon on your shirt or pullover and hold it 5 cm above the basket, touching the wall. Let go, saying, *'Stay!'* as you do so. The balloon will stay there.

WHAT HAPPENED
Rubbing the balloon scraped some electrons on to it, which gave it an electro-static charge. This made it attractive to the wall. It will stay there until the electrons have balanced out between the balloon and the wall.

CHAPTER 8
AIR SMILES

The next few magic marvels make use of invisible weights. There's about 80 Kg of invisible weight sitting on this book.

The wonder substance is air, of course. It is completely invisible and very light, but there's a lot of it, stretching over 40 miles up to the edge of space, so that is bound to add up to a pretty good weight. There it is then, 80 kg of it pressing on you from all sides, waiting to be used for some mystic marvels.

Like everything else, air is made of zillions of **atoms**, tiny tiny particles that bounce around in a vast throng. These atoms are seriously small. To give you an idea of the smallness of them, if all the atoms in a doughnut were enlarged to the size of grains of sand, we could see them – just about – but the doughnut would be the size of Spain!

When atoms get hot they bounce around more. So they each take up more space. So there are fewer atoms in a bucket of hot air than in a bucket of cold air. So it weighs less; it is less dense.

Put a bundle of hot, light air into a mass of colder, heavier air and it will float upwards in the same way that light objects float upwards in water. In other words, hot air rises! If you surround this bundle of hot air by a big paper bag; sling a basket underneath; put a duck, a rooster and a pig in the basket; and let go, you have a scene similar to the one that occurred in June 1783, when the Montgolfier brothers made man's very first flying machine: a hot air balloon. Two months later, a man rose off the face of the planet for the first time in over three million years of human evolution.

We can't match the magic of that event, but we can still do some pretty wonderful things.

MAGIC WINDMILL

One of the simplest tricks, yet one of the most amazing,
uses the fact that hot air rises.

THE EFFECT
The magician makes a piece of paper rotate purely by
willpower.

YOU NEED
•Piece of paper
•Pencil

TO PERFORM
This is a very delicate piece of magic, and needs to be done
in a quiet corner of a room, away from any kind of draught.

Tell your audience that you are hoping to become a spin
doctor. Ultimately, the aim is to affect the spin of the Earth,
making it go round faster during the week and slower on
Saturdays and Sundays, to give longer weekends. To begin
with, though, you must practise on pieces of paper.

While you are telling them all these fascinating personal
details, take any piece of paper and tear an oblong out of it,
about this size.

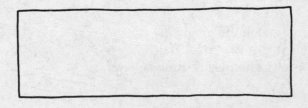

Fold it down the middle and across
the diagonal, as shown.

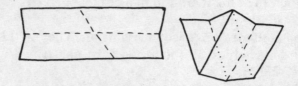

Balance the paper on the point of a
sharp pencil, right in the middle,
where the two folds cross.
Put on a look of deep, deep
concentration. Try to look
like this . . .

. . . and the paper
will do this . . .

WHAT HAPPENED

The source of energy is your hot hand. It warms the air above it, which rises and bounces into the angled piece of paper, pushing it around in a circle.

The audience can't see the rising air. They will look for hidden engines, elastic bands, mirrors, strings.

Why not let them have a go. They only thing to take care about is NOT TO BREATHE! At least don't breathe all over your delicate little windmill: you'll disrupt the 'engine'.

Light Blue

This magic uses water and can be messy.

THE EFFECT
At last we know why the sky is blue. The magician demonstrates that blue air rises.

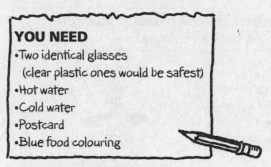

YOU NEED
- Two identical glasses
  (clear plastic ones would be safest)
- Hot water
- Cold water
- Postcard
- Blue food colouring

SECRET PREPARATION
Completely fill one glass with hot water, the other with cold. Put some drops of blue in the hot one.

TO PERFORM
Tell the audience about the miraculous discoveries of modern science:

1 wind is caused by all those trees waving about;

2 pigs can and do fly;

3 giraffes have long necks because otherwise their heads wouldn't be properly attached to their bodies; AND...

4 ...the sky is blue because blue air rises.

Hold the postcard on top of the blue glass and turn it over.

Place it over the other glass and carefully remove the card. The blue water will stay in the top glass.

Now – and this is something you need to practise over a sink – turn the whole lot over. The blue water will rise to the top again, proving that blue things are lighter than non-blue things: blue air rises!

> WARNING If this trick is done properly, scientific progress could be set back a thousand years.

WHAT HAPPENED
The blue water was indeed lighter than the ordinary water, because it was hotter. When it was on top, it stayed there. When it was swivelled to the bottom, it rose to the top again. Swivel it a few times and the waters will mix up to make a glass of warm, light blue water.

SPIRAL MOBILES

Use hot air power to make some sassy revolving decorations.

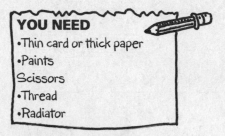

YOU NEED
- Thin card or thick paper
- Paints
- Scissors
- Thread
- Radiator

TO PERFORM
Cut the card into circles, then decorate them with bright colours.

Cut just over 1 cm into the circle, then turn and continue cutting round, keeping the same distance from the edge, until you are near the centre. You should end up with a spiral.

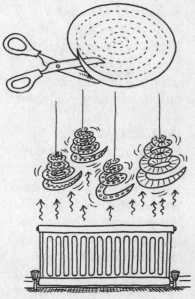

Attach a thread to the middle and hang the spiral over a radiator. It will spin gently round as the rising air bumps against the sloping surface. For the best effect, put several in a line.

INCIDENTALLY . . .

If you want to dry things out near the radiator, don't put them under it, because hot air only rises, it never takes time off to sink.

INCIDENTALLY . . .

Ever wondered how all the water in a kettle heats up, when the heating element is at the bottom? As the water at the bottom warms up, it rises, and cooler water is dragged in from the side, which is heated and rises . . . and so on.

INCIDENTALLY . . .

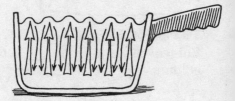

Ever wondered why saucepans of fat get a honeycomb pattern of lumps on the surface? It's caused by neighbouring columns of rising hot fat and descending cooler fat.

INCIDENTALLY . . .

Ever wondered what the surface of the sun looks like? Very similar to that pan of fat, but a wee bit hotter!

INCIDENTALLY . . .

Ever wondered how weather works? Very similar, only cooler! Clouds are formed when warmer air rises. Winds are caused when cooler air rushes in to replace it.

CHAPTER NINE
PAPER WORK

Paper was invented nearly 2,000 years ago in China, by Ts'ai Lun. It is still made in pretty much the same way today as it was then, and this gives us a chance to perform another piece of trickery.

✳ Magic ✳

RIPPING FUN

THE EFFECT
The magician can rip a straight strip off a newspaper; nobody else can.

YOU NEED
•A newspaper

TO PERFORM

Show the audience how easy it is to rip a straight line through a newspaper. When you've done a few, let someone try it; start the rip off for them, then let them continue. Their rip will be all over the place. Every time *you rip*, it's perfect. Every time *they try*, it's a mess.

This is the trick. Look carefully at the edges of the paper before you start. You must always start your rip from the zig-zag edge, but you must be sure they start theirs from the smooth edge.

WHAT HAPPENED

Paper is made from tiny fragments of wood, laid down as a pulp on a conveyor belt before being dried. As the conveyor belt moves, the fragments are stretched and straightened so that they all point the same way. When you rip in the direction of the fragments, the tear runs straight through. But try to tear across, and your tear is deflected by the fragments.

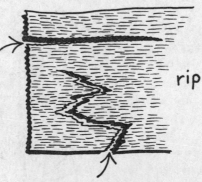

rip

MIGHTY PAPER

A demonstration of paper's strength.

THE EFFECT
The magician challenges anyone to balance this book on a piece of paper. When all have failed, the magician does it with ease.

YOU NEED
• This book
• Sheet of ordinary A4-sized paper

TO PERFORM
The challenge is to balance this book on the paper, edgewise. It seems impossible, but if you roll the paper up into a tube you can balance it easily – and 20 more, besides!

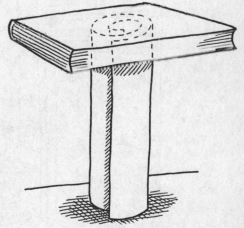

WHAT HAPPENED
Here you can see why tubes are the favourite shape for plant stems. They combine simplicity, strength and lightness, yet still allow the plant to sway in all directions.

PAPER PHOTOS

In Ts'ai Lun's day, paper was a pale brown colour. Recently, papermakers have taken to adding bleach to make it white, but the unfortunate side effect is that, in time, the bleach rots the paper – books published 10 years ago are in a worse state of decay than those printed 200 years ago. One of the signs of ageing is a browning of the paper. This happens in only a few days if the paper is in direct sunlight, so you can use it almost like photographic paper.

Put a pattern of coins on a piece of blank white paper and leave it in a place where it gets maximum sun and air. After a week of sunny days there will be a faint 'photo' of the coins' silhouettes on the paper.

PERFORMING UNDER PRESSURE

Before we can do the next two tricks, we need to get one or two things sorted:

1 Hot air rises, but not because it's hot! Hot air is less dense than the surrounding cool air, that's why it rises.

2 Actually, it doesn't rise at all. It gets pushed! Heavier air is pulled down harder towards the earth than lighter air (by gravity). As it is pulled down, it pushes the lighter stuff out of the way. The only place for the lighter air to go is upwards.

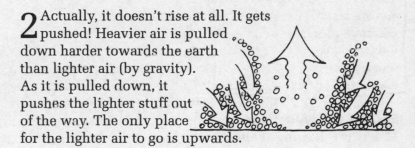

There is another way to make air lighter – get it moving!

What happens when humans get moving? When a marathon race begins, all the runners spread out. The same things happens to the atoms of air when the air gets moving. So moving air is lighter than still air.

Now you're ready to blow their minds away.

BAD PAPER

THE EFFECT
When the magician orders pieces of paper to be disobedient, they obediently disobey.

YOU NEED
- Paper
- Card
- Sellotape
- Drinking straw
- Drawing pin
- Cotton reel

SECRET PREPARATION
Make the following shapes.

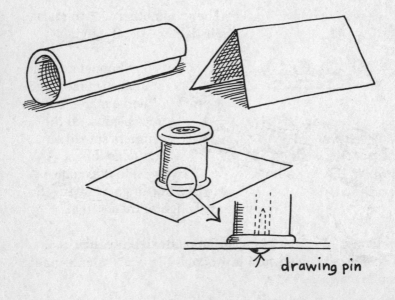

drawing pin

TO PERFORM

Line up the pieces of paper etc. in front of you and order them to disobey you. Command them to do the opposite of everything you say.

Firstly, hold up two pieces of paper face to face, as in the picture. Say, '*I shall now blow you apart.*' Blow between them. As they move together, say, '*Good!*'

Place the paper loop on the table. Say, '*I shall blow on your back to make you come towards me.*' Use the straw to blow across the back as shown – the loop will roll away.

Set up the tent. Say, '*I shall blow the sides of the tent outwards.*' Blow through the tent – it will bend inwards.

Hold a single sheet of paper flat below your mouth. Say, '*I shall blow you away.*' Blow across the top while the paper bends upwards.

Finally, pick up the card and cotton reel. Say, '*Finally, I shall blow this piece of card down to the floor.*' Blow through the cotton reel. For as long as you blow, the card will stay there.

WHAT HAPPENED

In all these cases the blowing of air made the air lighter, or less dense. The heavier, denser air moved in on it, carrying any neighbouring piece of paper with it.

Chimneys rely on the same trick. Wind blowing across the top of the chimney is lighter than the air further down, which is forced upwards by the pressure from the denser air in the room below.

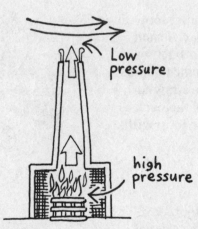

The grandest display of this use of **atmospheric pressure** is in the magic of flight . . .

FLIGHTS OF FANCY

Humans have wanted to fly since forever. Stories of angels with wings, gods in flying chariots, Daedalus and Icarus etc are peppered through every country's myths.

But in spite of all the beetle-browed study that went into it, nobody got a handle on how to do it until 100 years ago. So if flight seems a confusing miracle to you, fear not, you are in the company of Galileo, Leonardo da Vinci, Archimedes, Newton, and all the greats up to Wilbur and Orville Wright – who actually cracked it in 1903 with the first heavier-than-air flight.

As the wing of an aeroplane slices through the sky, the air runs over the top and under the bottom. But because of the curve on the top of the wing, the air has to go a little bit faster over the top than underneath. Because it goes faster, it becomes slightly less dense, so the pressure on the bottom of the wing is higher than that on the top, so the wing is pushed upwards.

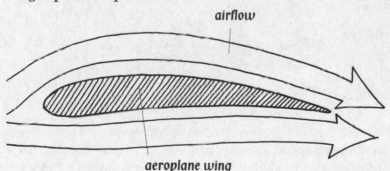

airflow

aeroplane wing

The idea seems so simple, but it was a long time coming.

THE POWER OF PAPER

That mass of air over our heads gives us another miracle.

THE EFFECT
The strongest person in the room is defeated by a piece of paper.

YOU NEED
•Newspaper
•Ruler

TO PERFORM
Arrange the ruler at the edge of the table, just so.

Ask the strongest person in the room if they can catapult it into the air by bashing the end. (Be very careful – there's no knowing where it will go.)

Now ask them if they think they could do the same with a single sheet of newspaper on the end. They should say yes.

Arrange the sheet over the ruler, as in the picture. Press it flat, then tell them to give the ruler a mighty thwack.

The paper will be unmoved; the ruler will stay there. The volunteer will be crestfallen. Beaten by a piece of paper! They'll never live it down!

WHAT HAPPENED

Air pressure pushes in all directions, so normally, there's 80 kg bearing down on top of the paper, – but also pushing up from underneath, so it all balances out.

When the ruler forces the paper upwards it creates a space where there is no air at all (a vacuum). With no air below it and 80 kg of air above it, there's no contest – the paper is forced down again, and the ruler with it.

It seems that the volunteer is defeated by the entire atmosphere. They shouldn't be too upset.

MAGICAL LIE-IN

HOW TO GET AN EXTRA HOUR IN BED

So now you know what to do when they scream up at you about it being nine-thirty, and when are you going to get to school. Tell them about the 80 kg weight pressing you down into your bed. They can't possibly expect you to struggle against that! (To say nothing of the 20 million dust mites waiting to pounce on you as soon as you touch the carpet.)

Meanwhile, sweet dreams!

LIST OF MAGIC TRICKS